Uninvited Guests
Living With Intrusive Voices

Sarah Clarke

Print ISBN: 978-1-09839-084-6

eBook ISBN: 978-1-09839-085-3

First Edition

"God grant me the serenity to accept the people I cannot change,
the courage to change the one I can,
and the wisdom to know it's me."

(Variation of the Serenity prayer, Author unknown)

"Ring the bells that still can ring
Forget your perfect offering
There is a crack, a crack in everything
That's how the light gets in."

Leonard Cohen from "Anthem"

TABLE OF CONTENTS

Preface ix

1. The Early Years 1

2. The Whispers 7

3. The Voices 11

4. The Next Phase (Spring 2012) 20

5. Pretending all is Fine (2013) 22

6. Theories... 24

7. Quickly Changing Moods 27

8. The Haldol Years (2014 – 2015)................................... 31

9. Observances of a Butterfly 35

10. OCD and Bags 39

11. The Hills Are Alive! 41

12. Potato Chip Wars... 43

13. Eleanor Longden 46

14. Heart Disease, GERD and Nagging 48

15. Loosening the Reins 50

16. The Sun 52

17. People and Quilts... 57

18. Cory has always wanted to be… 59

19. Cory is Back!... 63

20. Acceptance (2021)... 66

21. Stigma 69

22. Finding the Right Doctor 73

23. Addendum 75

Acknowledgements 78

Preface

All parents struggle and worry when their children face difficult challenges, illnesses or injuries. When a child is born with a permanent disability the issues parents face are multiplied ten-fold. Our son, Cory, was born with cerebral palsy and later developed epilepsy, but it was the diagnosis of schizophrenia at age 19 that really complicated our lives.

Over the years I sought counseling from different professionals to help me cope with the stresses of life with a multiply-challenged child. In September of 2016, five years after Cory's schizophrenia diagnosis, I stumbled on a writing class called "Writing Out of Your Life" at the Jewish Community Center in New City, New York. The teacher was Lynn Lauber, author of "*White Girls*," and "*Listen to Me, Writing Life into Meaning*." Her philosophy of writing was to write instinctively without censoring or judging, no editing or crossing out. Just to write whatever comes into your head and get it down as fast as possible. She even suggested using "fast writing" pens. For me the class became another form of therapy. I found I wanted to share my stories, and writing them down helped me understand myself more and accept how my life had changed.

In the class we wrote on prompts that Lynn gave us every week and those prompts sparked a flood of memories, all the way from my own childhood up through the present day. After the class Lynn invited me to join a writer's group that met weekly to share stories. As you can imagine, a lot of my stories centered around our son Cory. After several years of meetings one of the writers in the group suggested I put all my "Cory" stories together, as they might be a useful resource for other families dealing with mental health issues and specifically schizophrenia. This book is a compilation of all those stories, woven together. Of course, every person and situation is unique and what we experienced and our struggles and solutions may not resonate with everyone.

Before diving in I think it is important to give some background about Cory and the specific circumstances that make his life unique.

1. The Early Years

Eric and I were married on September 8th, 1986. We had been living busy lives as freelance musicians in New York City, playing in local orchestras and touring the country and the world as members of the Orpheus Chamber Orchestra. It was a second marriage for both of us and we wanted to have children right away, since we were in our thirties. My first pregnancy was an ectopic and after that nothing happened for five years. Multiple fertility treatments later we decided to try IVF (*In Vitro Fertilization*). Back in the 1980s it was a very expensive and new procedure, only 15 or 20 years old. A doctor at New York Hospital was recommended and we began the grueling routine of early morning trips to the hospital, leaving the house at 5:30 AM to get there by 7:00 AM for blood tests, hormone shots and sonograms.

Our first cycle was a failure but we had just enough money for a second try. More early-morning trips to the city, shots, tests and sonograms, but this time we were successful. Cory was born on May 25, 1991, in Englewood, New Jersey. He was supposed to be born in early July but

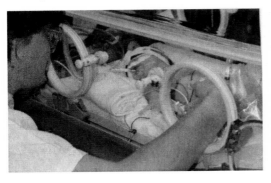

my water broke and he came six weeks early. Our doctor was able to measure his thighbone in a sonogram and determine that he was big, at least 6 lbs. 4 oz., and decided it was safe to induce labor. He thought perhaps the due date was off and was sure he was ready. Cory was in fact 6 lbs. 4 oz., but his lungs were not fully developed and he quickly went into respiratory distress. Englewood Hospital did not have a neonatal intensive care unit at that time so Cory was put into an oxygen tent for eight hours until a team from New York's Mount Sinai Hospital could come out and intubate him. Then he was transferred by ambulance to Mount Sinai where he stayed in an incubator, intubated, until he was able to breathe on his own.

We looked at our precious child, for whom we had waited so long, with so many tubes attached for oxygen and blood draws. Eric and I reached into the incubator through the rubberized armholes, touching and stroking our son, giving some small contact of love and connection. It was frightening how helpless and vulnerable he looked. After a week Cory came out of the incubator and I was able to try to feed him. After ten days we took him home.

Over the course of the next year Cory failed to reach his milestones on time. At six months he still could not sit up without support. By one year he had not learned to crawl or roll over. The pediatrician was reassur-

ing at first, telling us that all preemies take a bit longer to catch up, but by a year it seemed clear that something neurological might be amiss. Cory's left eye had begun to wander and the eye doctor suggested that we see a neurologist, as she couldn't perceive any muscular or vision problem. We had Cory examined by a pediatric developmental specialist at St. Joseph's Children's Hospital. He determined that Cory had cerebral palsy, a traumatic brain injury, which occurred shortly before, during, or shortly after birth, and was the result of a lack of oxygen to the brain. We were devastated and imagined that Cory

2

would never walk, talk, feed himself, live independently, go to college or get married. His whole life flew in front of our eyes and it seemed hopeless and sad. But then the doctor reassured us that Cory's case seemed mild to moderate, and with therapy he could live a very normal and productive life. He recommended a program at Hackensack University Medical Center called "The Institute for Child Development" and that is where we went for the next 18 years for Cory's therapy. He got physical therapy, speech therapy, occupational therapy and also educational testing by their child study team, who then made recommendations to his teachers at school.

Cory learned to walk at age four, the summer after his first year at P.I.E. (Preschool Instruction for the Exceptional). He then went to the regular public school in our town of Norwood, New Jersey. Early on it was determined that he had substantial learning differences and he was put into some special-ed classes.

At age five Cory was diagnosed with *Benign Rolandic Epilepsy*, a kind of epilepsy where the seizures are mild and only happen when a child is drifting off to sleep or just waking up. The neurologist did not recommend medicating him as there was no danger of injury, and he said it would likely disappear when Cory reached puberty.

By fifth grade Cory was in a self-contained special-ed class, except for music, art and gym. He had various tutors over the years, some during the school year and some over the summer months, to keep him from losing ground. They all fell in love with our delightful son and he still keeps in touch with several of them through letters.

Cory was a very happy child and never seemed frustrated or angry about his disability. In fact he rarely questioned us about it. We waited for years for him to come to us for answers about why he was different, why he couldn't run or climb or read like the other kids. It hardly ever happened and only this once did he express his anger and frustration: Cory was ten. My sister Lindy and her son Jesse (age 11 at the time) were at our house for breakfast one weekend. Cory had climbed up the stairs to his room to get dressed. When he pulled open the top drawer of his bureau to get out a T-shirt, he lost his balance. Holding onto the drawer as he started to fall backwards, he pulled the entire bureau down on top of himself. We all heard the crash from downstairs and raced up to find him pinned underneath the wooden bureau. Cory was very frightened and was crying out for help. We lifted the bureau off him and helped him up. One ankle was twisted but nothing was broken. He cried for 30 or 40 minutes, asking many times, "Why do I have CP?" We tried to calm him down with lame expressions about bad luck and getting dealt a rotten hand of cards, but trying your best to play that hand anyway. It wasn't much comfort for a ten year-old boy.

At age 15 Cory's physical challenges had become such that an orthopedic surgery was necessary to keep his hips from going out of their sockets and to straighten his legs, which were extremely turned in at the knees. The surgeon performed a quadruple, bilateral osteotomy. He cut the thighbones just below the hip and rotated both legs out, which left his feet turned out to each side. He then cut his lower leg bones at the ankle and rotated his feet back to face straight forward again. This surgery was extremely challenging for Cory. He was "bed to chair" for three months and then had to learn to walk again, which took another three months. He went from a walker to two crutches and finally to one *Lofstrand* (forearm) crutch, which he still uses today.

After this surgery Cory had his first *grand mal* seizure. At first we thought it was an anomaly caused by a sudden decrease in the muscle relaxer, *Ativan*, which he had been taking post-surgery. But three years

4

later he had another seizure and then they started coming with more and more frequency. By the time he graduated from high school the seizures had snowballed from one, to two, to four a year. We knew this was not terribly frequent by some epileptic's standards, who can experience multiple seizures in a day, but it was enough to put us on edge, not knowing when the next one would occur. Cory would fall down and convulse out of the blue, just walking to the door, or fall off the toilet while peeing, or collapse at the breakfast table. The seizures came without warning and we were afraid to leave him alone for fear of a life-threatening head injury or asphyxiation, choking on his own spit or vomit.

Several times the outcome could have been disastrous if we hadn't been right there. Once, sitting at the breakfast island he started screaming, "Bad! Really bad!" over and over, pointing to his head where he was feeling excruciating pain. Seconds later he was in full convulsions, after we caught him from falling on the hard stone floor. We had been taught by the neurologist to roll him onto his side to keep him from choking and to put a pillow under his head to protect it. Cory never had any memories of his seizures. The only evidence was a splitting headache and the pain on the side of his tongue where his chattering jaw had chewed it raw.

Hope that Cory would overcome many of his physical issues was always uppermost in our minds. We tried everything the therapists recommended, doing exercises every day at home before he even went to school, stretching and strengthening for at least a half an hour. A family friend helped us install rope railings up at our summer camp in Maine so Cory could climb down the steep and rocky path to the back dock and ride in the boat; good therapy! We hung a swinging platform in our living room and a tire swing from the oak tree in the backyard for more physical therapy disguised as fun. We bought him a recumbent trike from an Australian company, *Greenspeed*. Amazingly, they were willing to design a new small-size trike just for Cory and he rode that trike for years, getting some good exercise and leg strength. However, when he started at the huge regional high school, we had to buy him an electric mobility scooter. The distances between classes were too long and he could easily have been knocked over in the rush of students in the hallways. All his grammar school years he had physical therapy two or three times a week, and in high school once a week, with the wonderful therapists at Hackensack Medical Center's Institute for Child Development.

There is even a documentary about Cory, created by his beloved physical therapist, Patti Ryan, who worked with Cory for all those years. Patti counseled us through all of his hospitalizations and even came to our house for therapy sessions when he was still house bound, post-surgery. We are forever in her debt.

Cory did graduate from high school, but the child study team and his guidance counselor recommended that he stay an extra "super senior" year, as no one felt he was ready to go to college yet.

And this is where the rest of the story begins.

2. The Whispers

"When did the whispering begin?" Cory's psychiatrist, Dr. Singh, asked us. It was in the early days of his schizophrenia diagnosis and often Cory was too anxious and paranoid to speak with the doctor so Eric and I would talk with him first and then Cory would join us later. I was puzzled....whispering? Since the beginning I could only remember Cory's voices being loud, threatening, scary, and abusive. He never talked about whispers......or had he? I got a sick, sinking feeling in my stomach as a dim light began to flicker in my memory.

Two years earlier, in 2010, when Cory was 18 and in his last year of high school, there was an incident that involved the choir. It was also  the year that Cory told us he was gay. It was a stressful year for him. He had gone for counseling with the pastor of our church, also a gay man, and had confided in him. The pastor encouraged Cory to be honest with us. We'd noticed the way he watched our handsome, young choir director at church, how he got up super early in the morning to fix his hair, gooping it up with product to look especially dashing every day before school, and all the little ways he showed absolutely no interest in girls at 18. So it was not a surprise to hear him finally blurt out his secret. We had seen this coming a mile away.

That year both we, and our pastor tried to support Cory in his new identity. After Cory told him he would like to meet some other gay teens his age, the pastor started a monthly get-together at our church called the Rainbow Café. It was, and still is ten years later, a chaperoned gathering for LGBTQ high school-aged kids to meet and get to know each other. It created a supportive and caring community for these youngsters, who can often feel isolated and bullied. Cory went once. It was too exciting, too highly charged with sexual undercurrent and, at that stage of his development, scary and overwhelming. Our pastor also found Cory a friend, a boy who was gay. We actually met this young man who went to a different church but had come to the Rainbow Café. He was a sweet guy and very friendly and warm towards Cory. We all went to a Messiah Sing together and the two boys sat next to each other. That also was too much for Cory. His friend's small hints of affection, a pat on the leg, bump of the shoulders, a hug goodbye, increased Cory's anxiety.

In school his fear of being found out was building. We had encouraged him to attend the Gay-Straight Alliance meetings but he refused. He had become enamored of a clique of boys in the choir and wanted desperately to join their group. He tried chatting them up, inviting them over, sitting with them at lunch, but they were not interested, reluctant, perhaps, to have their group disrupted by a SPED (Special-Ed) kid with a lopsided gait. They were the cool kids in the choir and the theater department, the stars of the shows!

This is when the whispering began. One day Cory came home from school and told me he was upset and worried because the boys in the choir were whispering about him.

"They sit behind me and I can hear them. They know I'm gay," he told me.

"Well, what are they saying?" I asked.

"Stuff like, 'How can you stand sitting right behind him? Gross. He's so weird.' Or 'Geez, look at him, see how he stares at Ryan…?' "

These are the kinds of whispers he heard. This went on for a few more days and Eric and I debated if we should say something to the teacher. Around that same time I had an unnerving experience, which corroborated Cory's story and cemented my decision to talk to the choir director. At a doctor's appointment I ran into the mother of two girls in the choir. She recognized me as Cory's Mom and asked if he was going on the spring trip, when the choir competes in a national competition. I explained,

"No, he has opted not to go. It would be impossible without an aide and he is nervous about flying."

"Does he enjoy the choir?" she asked.

"Yes," I replied "He loves to sing and it's a great choir, way better than our church choir, and he likes the director very much."

"That's interesting," she hesitantly replied. I looked puzzled and so she continued.

"Because my girls say everyone in the choir is mean to Cory." For a moment I didn't think I had heard right.

"All the kids are mean to him," she repeated. I felt a surge of anger rises up in my chest.

"Well that's pretty sad," I said, "but luckily I don't think Cory is much affected by it. He hasn't mentioned it to me." But as I drove home I stewed and stewed. I will tell the teacher, she should know what's going on, I decided.

In the end it was a disaster all around. The teacher told the vice-principal. Then there had to be an inquiry into this accusation of bullying. The parents were called. Cory had to identify the boys. They denied it all and were outraged, "falsely accused," they said. The vice-principal told them they had to apologize and be on good behavior or be removed from the choir. They opted to quit the choir.

After that the entire choir turned against Cory. No one would speak to him. His cheerful "Good Morning!" was met with silence. After a month or so of this deafening wall of shunning he quit the choir as well. To this day we still wonder, were the whispers actually in his head, the sinister start of his voices? Or were they just mean kids, whispering about someone who is different?

3. The Voices

About a year later, in the fall of 2011, came the complete psychotic break-down. Cory was out of school, trying to find things to do to keep busy. He wanted a paying job but with his physical limitations it was impossible to find anything that suited his abilities. He was volunteering at a library nearby, organizing the movies into alphabetical order and re-shelving mag-azines, and finding even that stressful. None of this was his strength and he began to worry. One afternoon I picked him up from the library and he told me that he was afraid to say certain words because people might misunderstand and be upset.

"Like what?" I asked.

"I was telling the head librarian that I had finished sorting some DVDs, and I…Oh No! That's what I can't say!"

It took me a few tries to finally understand what he meant. He was afraid to say "and I" for fear that someone would mistake it for "and die," as if he was threatening the librarian. This kind of paranoid thinking became worse as Cory's anxiety grew more intense. More words were taboo, more people were looking at him strangely.

During his last year in high school Cory had taken a course called "Constitutional and Street Law." It was taught by a retired police officer. In that course he had learned the scary statistics of innocent people who were incarcerated. He started talking about getting in trouble for something he didn't do and was increasingly worried that he would be arrested. We con-sulted a psychiatrist and our neurologist. We began trying medications but the snowball had begun rolling and there seemed no way to stop it.

I'm not sure when it finally dawned on us that Cory was hearing things that weren't there. He had begun to live in an alternate reality. Cory began to notice cars with their headlights coming down the street at night. He believed they were coming for him, to arrest him. If a car's light shone in the window he believed it was a policeman outside with a flashlight searching for evidence against him. He heard people talking outside in the yard, saying scary things. They were always talking **about** him and this is one of the idiosyncrasies of Cory's voices. They talk about him to each other but never directly to him. They say, "He's going to be arrested" or "He will get sick and die."

We tried to reason with him, saying, "These are voices in your head, they are not real." But they sounded as real to him as we did. At night he would hear people downstairs in our kitchen. "They are taking finger-prints off our glasses, Mom. They say I'm going to be arrested." My brother, Michael, was a special agent in the FBI and Cory started calling him daily.

"Uncle Michael, can you call the Norwood police and tell them I'm not the one they want, they've made a mistake?" My brother played along. He said he would call.

"Don't worry, I'll take care of it."

Of course he didn't call. We were grasping at anything that would calm his worries, but they couldn't be calmed. Once the neurotransmitters start sending out that fight-or-flight hormone, without the proper amount of medication to tamp it down, it is like a huge river rushing toward the ocean. It starts with little streams feeding into it and then more, larger streams pour in and finally it swells into a monster, gushing and racing along, and nothing can stop its destructive course. Later we learned that all our tactics to try and help Cory were totally the wrong thing. I will explain that in another chapter.

One night in early January 2011, Cory snapped. His brain became overwhelmed with the fear of what these voices were saying. He ran into our bedroom at 3:00 AM in a complete panic. "Mom! Dad! I've just been informed that I will be put to death by lethal injection this morning at 10:00 AM!"

We tried to calm him, get him to take some anti-anxiety medication. We sat him on the couch and then slowly we realized he was not talking anymore. His eyes were staring straight ahead and he couldn't open his mouth to swallow a pill or even water. We desperately called one doctor after another, the psychiatrist, the neurologist, even our family doctor. The neurologist, Dr. Jacobson, was the first to call us back.

"Are his arms frozen up in the air, stiff?" he asked.

"Yes," we said. "They can't seem to relax. We keep trying to push them down but they just go up again."

"He's become catatonic. Take him to the hospital and go to New York, not a New Jersey hospital. Go to Columbia Presbyterian, it's the best one that's close to you," he told us.

Now we were in a full-blown panic. Catatonic? What does that mean? Cory couldn't move. His body was like wood, inflexible. I don't know how Eric managed to carry him out to the car. I dragged along the wheelchair and shoved it in the back and we raced, hearts pounding, to New York City.

The hospital was a zoo, and it seemed like an eternity before Cory was seen by an Emergency Room doctor. Twice he broke out of the catatonic state and tried to run away and Eric had to grab him and carry him back to the examining cubicle. He was terrified and didn't understand why we were forcing him to stay there. He was in a delusional state where everyone was trying to hurt him or take him away to prison or worse. Who knows what his voices were screaming inside his head. Finally, after a lengthy discussion with the ER doctor, Cory was admitted to the children's neurologic unit. Even though he was 19 at the time, the doctor could see that he was developmentally younger than his actual age. We have always been grateful that they did not place him in the adult psychiatric ward, which could have been extremely frightening for him. A security guard was stationed outside his room because he was considered a flight risk, aggravating his paranoia of being watched by the police, but the staff members were kind and very attentive. Since it was a children's ward we were allowed to stay with Cory all day and sleep there at night.

Cory was in the hospital for 16 days and half of that time he completely lost his ability to speak, to move, to eat or swallow. We were petrified that our son would never come back. Both Eric and I cried a lot, but we always took turns, leaving the room or turning toward the window so that Cory would not see how scared we were. The doctors explained that to calm his brain they would have to give him massive amounts of *Ativan*, a benzodiazepine, which increases the production of the calming hormone in the brain called *Gamma-Aminobutyric acid* (GABA). This counterbalances the fight-or-flight hormone, which had gone berserk in Cory's brain. But *Ativan* can, when given in high doses, calm your brain so much that you can stop breathing, so Cory had to be on all sorts of monitors and alarms that went off at all hours of the day and night when his oxygen level went too low.

We looked at our son and saw the panic in his eyes. It was clear he could hear us and understand what the doctors were saying but he had no ability to move or respond. Often it was clear he wanted something but we had no idea what, and this was frustrating and upsetting for all of us. The doctors tried to explain to us what had happened in Cory's brain to cause the catatonia. Apparently it is a state of shock that is caused by emotional trauma and extreme fear, real or imagined, rather than physical trauma. Cory's brain began putting out more and more of the fight-or-flight hormones *glutamate* and *norepinephrine*, as the voices revved and a vicious merry-go-round began to spin. The louder and more frequent the voices became, the more of these fight-or-flight hormones poured into his brain. The neurotransmitter that produces the calming hormone, GABA, could not keep up and everything got out of balance. Finally it was too much for his brain to handle. As a protective mechanism the brain can shut itself down before it explodes or too much damage occurs. But when the brain shuts down, as it does after an epileptic seizure, the whole body shuts down too. All the connections from the brain to the body are cut off, nothing works. The brain is in control of all one's movements. If there is no signal, there is no muscular function. This is catatonia. Cory was frozen in a body that could not respond while his mind was still on high alert.

Then a miracle came from my dear friend, Sue Lorentsen. She remembered hearing that stroke victims who have lost the ability to speak, move or write can still squeeze with their hands. "Try it with Cory," she suggested. And we did. We would ask a question. "Are you thirsty? Squeeze my hand for yes, let go for no." It worked! He was able to squeeze! And that was our lifeline for the next week or more until he slowly and determinedly began to recover his speech and movements.

At one point my brother Michael, the FBI agent, was visiting. He is a very tough guy on the outside but has a soft, caring heart on the inside. He is used to fixing problems and fighting hard for causes he believes in. He worried that if no one was right next to Cory's bed to hold his hand that he would not be able to get anyone's attention should he need something. It was driving Michael crazy and he seemed like a trapped animal, pacing the room as he tried to come up with a solution. Finally he got an idea and ran out into the street. He came back with a toy that would squeak when squeezed, a little feathery duck, small enough to fit in Cory's hand. It worked and Cory used it for the next week until he could speak again.

We moved the couch on which we slept right next to Cory's hospital bed and Eric, who spent most nights there, slept with his hand holding Cory's all night long, protective and loving. If Cory woke up and was frightened or needed something, Eric would feel that squeeze and wake up to help him.

Cory slowly inched his way out of the catatonic state. He spoke single words at first, almost in slow motion and with great effort. It took him two minutes or more to take a sip of water and force his reluctant throat muscles to swallow it. When he was finally able to croak out a few words, a nurse began coming every day to test his cognitive awareness. She wanted to assess his ability to understand reality and also learn how deep and pervasive were his delusions. She always asked the same questions:

Do you know where you are?

Do you know who I am?

Do you know who that is? (Pointing to me or Eric)

Do you know why you are here?

What's your name?

Cory's first real answer to the question, "Do you know where you are?" was "Venezuela." The nurse seemed to think this was not a good sign, but we knew how Cory's mind worked and explained that we thought he was struggling to come up with the name of the hospital, Columbia Presbyterian. He knew it was the name of a South American country but Venezuela was the first name he came up with. Far more disturbing was his response to the question, "Why are you here?" His first answer was, "Because someone is going to kill my father." A day or two later his response to that same question was, "To remove the defecation from my brain." We thought that was a very apt description of why he was there in the hospital! Only Cory, even under these most frightening and debilitating circumstances, would take the time to use a more polite word in place of "shit." Cory has been, and always will be, a most polite and proper guy. I've never heard him utter the "F" word, even though he's heard it from me on many occasions.

One day a doctor came by who was a catatonia specialist. He had been practicing for over 20 years and told us that in all those years he had only seen three other cases of full blown catatonia, it was that rare. He was so curious to ask Cory, what did it feel like? He wondered, did Cory feel slowed down in a world that was swirling and speeding around him? Or was it the opposite? That the world around him was moving at a snail's pace but his mind was racing? I don't think he ever got a full answer. It was too hard to put into words.

Many times, as Cory recovered, he would reach out both arms to us in a desperate need to be held and reassured. He often asked that we keep him safe and not let him die. But there was also an element of love and gratitude that we had shielded and protected him, and this reaching out in the most childlike way was so touching and sad.

The doctors asked us what Cory's normal speech was like. A person with cerebral palsy often has very little ability to speak or move. They wanted to wait until he was close to his normal level of functioning before releasing him from the hospital. We tried to explain that Cory could walk independently and that his speech was very fluent and he had a great vocabulary. This was hard for them to imagine, considering the condition he was in at that moment. So Eric had the brilliant idea to call our home answering machine where Cory had recorded the outgoing message. They were astounded to hear his voice, strong and clear, rattling off our message.

"Hello, you've reached the Bartlett residence. No one is available to take your call. Please leave a message at the beep and someone will call you back as soon as possible. Thanks, and have a blessed day!" Now the doctors knew what their goal was. He reached it on day 16.

All through those 16 days of Cory's stay at Columbia Presbyterian our friends and family were there to support us. I can't stress enough how important that was to Cory's recovery and to our mental health. Nick and Gina, our nephew and his wife who were doctoral students in the city, came almost every day bringing food. Cory's voice teacher, Cheryl, and her husband, Glenn, came when Cory was enough improved to croak out a few notes and Cheryl played her electric piano and sang some songs with him. Other friends came bringing stuffed animals, music CDs and always food for us. My sister, Lindy, came every other day and her son Jesse came up from The College of New Jersey. Uncle John had a layover at JFK and rode the subway for an hour and a half each way, dragging his suitcase the whole time, to stop in for a short visit. One time when Jesse and his Dad were there, they showed Cory a silly cell phone game called "Talking Tom." It changes your voice to a high squeak, like a mouse, and it got Cory to try talking more.

My brother Michael and his wife, Maryrose, came up from Florida and stayed in a nearby hotel for a week. Maryrose is a nurse and she happened to be there when Cory was having a spinal tap. Cory was being held in an uncomfortable fetal position so his spine was rounded. There were several doctors and a handful of interns crowding around his bed to watch the procedure. Afterwards, the attending doctor asked for "the band-aid" and no one had one. There was a flurry of questions,

"Who's got the band-aid, where's the band-aid? I know I had a band-aid....!"

No one seemed capable of finding a band-aid. Maryrose jumped up and ran out calling,

"I'll get a band-aid!" She stormed the nurse's station, got them to open the supply closet and returned a minute later waving the band-aid high over her head calling out,

"I've got the band-aid!"

When Cory was discharged he was on all sorts of new medications, two anti-psychotics, an anti-anxiety medication, and his usual anticonvulsant. We were hopeful that this episode was a one-time thing and that now that he had the right medications it would never happen again. Life would go back to normal. How naïve we were...

4. The Next Phase (Spring 2012)

The voices were gone for quite a while after that first hospital stay. We actually began to relax a little. Cory's physical weakness from the catatonia disappeared and his speech returned to normal. But about six weeks after his discharge he began to hear the voices again. Our hearts sank as it dawned on us that it wasn't over, that we might be facing another round of this, the worst nightmare of our lives as parents. We had already faced Cory's birth as a preemie, his diagnosis of cerebral palsy one year later, and his first epileptic seizure at age 15. But all these challenges seemed like a bike ride in the park compared to the onset of schizophrenia and his descent into catatonia. Would it happen again? We had so many questions. Was he on the right medication? Was it at the right level? How do we get him to understand that these voices he is hearing are not real? How do we explain to him what is going on in his brain? Sadly, the doctors were not terribly forthcoming with us. "Busier is better" was practically all the advice they gave us. "The more he is engaged in other activities and his brain is occupied with thinking about other things, the less the voices have a chance to push through and take over."

At first Cory was not able to participate in any outside activity. Anything outside the safety of our home was too scary. So we devised our own plan; we brought activities to him. He had voice lessons at home, since we have a piano. A Spanish tutor came to the house once a week. We hired caregivers to come for several hours a day to give me a break. They would play cards, bake cookies, take him out for pizza, or read books together and watch a TV show.

In the fall of 2012, as the voices decreased, we dared to sign him up for a semester at the community college. That was a total failure. Too much anxiety, too many strange people, too much pressure. The only class he really enjoyed was the chorus. He dropped out after the fall semester.

We tried a mental health daycare center where we hoped he would meet other people with similar issues. There were group therapies, and art and music periods which all sounded good to us. But the staff was over-stretched and the clients there all had very debilitating mental health problems as well. Most of them were stuck in their very paranoid or delusional worlds and unable to relate to each other. Cory went to this program twice a week for a year with no measurable improvement.

Meanwhile, with the help of Cory's psychiatrist, we were trying different cocktails of medications. Over the first seven years we must have tried ten different antipsychotics and three different anticonvulsants, plus two different anti-anxiety meds. None of them proved to be all that effective no matter how high the dose.

We began to realize that being with mentally healthy people was going to be better for Cory than in a group program for people with mental illness, and keeping him busy with activities at home and in our own town, where he had come to feel safe, was going to help him the most. But it meant that our lives were going to be hugely changed, having Cory home with us all the time.

5. Pretending all is Fine (2013)

From the start Eric and I had tried to keep Cory from seeing our own fears about his illness. It seemed that it could only exacerbate his anxiety. But boy was that hard, trying to pretend everything is okay when it isn't by a long shot! It is so much work to put on an easy, carefree front when your child is spinning down into a paranoid and delusional state. But for me to show my anxiety and sadness was not helpful. I wanted the first voice that Cory heard in the morning when he woke up to be mine, a real person, not the delusional ones in his head, to keep him in touch with reality. So I started singing whenever I heard him beginning to stir each morning. I would breeze into his room with a tune on my lips, opening his curtains with "Down in the Valley" or "You Are My Sunshine." I wanted him to see that the world is a good place, and the things he was worried about were not going to come true.

His fears ranged from some silly, annoying things that the voices were talking about to much more dire circumstances. It slowly became clear to us that his voices were almost all women and that they only talked to each other, never directly to him. At times a voice would say, "Someone is going to steal his tea kettle," or "He'll never drink another cup of coffee." Or if they got louder and more threatening they would convince Cory of more frightening things. "He will be arrested. He's going to get sick and not be able to breathe."

These fears probably had some root in his own feeling of vulnerability. He knew he was declining physically. Little by little, as the doctor upped his medication, the weaker and less physically stable he became.

He couldn't walk as well anymore, fell more often and had to use a walker frequently. He began to slump to the side when sitting on the couch and this caused more and more gastric reflux and damage to his esophagus. He started to drool and couldn't keep his eyes open.

Eric and I worried about these things but we both pretended that everything was fine. Life is good! There's so much to look forward to! I was constantly making desperate attempts to pull my son back to reality, to a happy family. "Let's sing a song, play some cards, go out shopping, bake some cookies or you can help me make a quilt!"

(This is the quilt we painstakingly made together out of his collection of bandanas. He didn't have much fun.)

I wasn't sure if I was helping but I know I was exhausting myself in hopes that my forced cheerfulness could somehow combat this disease that was ebbing and flowing in and out of our son's brain. It was not possible to sit by and watch Cory turn from his wonderful, funny, lovable self into a fearful, suspicious person, retreating from his family and the world.

6. Theories

There are a lot of theories out there about what causes schizophrenia and when we heard that fateful word for the first time we went right to the Internet. In hindsight it was not the smartest thing to do, but a parent with little knowledge about what's going wrong in their child's brain is more than a bit desperate.

I read a lot of things, some that were valid and others not. One theory that I read on the Internet suggested that an overbearing parent, a mother or father who is constantly telling their child what to do and making all his choices for him, can cause a crisis of identity. Children who have no self-esteem or any idea who they are can become severely anxious when they are finally out on their own and having to make choices for themselves. The pressure of it is overwhelming and can cause a psychotic breakdown. I worried that I had in fact *caused* Cory to go off the rails and become schizophrenic. Had I been too controlling? Because of his physical disability we had planned all of his daily activities. He had physical therapy, occupational therapy, tutors and social skills classes. We had taken him to a myriad of doctors and therapists for tests and surgeries, trying to find solutions for his epileptic seizures, his physical issues and learning problems. It seemed plausible that we had robbed him of his self-confidence. How could he not think something was really wrong with him?

Our family doctor has a sign on her wall that says, "Please don't confuse your Google search with my medical degree!" I wish I had seen that sign the year Cory had his breakdown. I could have saved myself a lot of needless worry.

After talking to many psychiatrists and psychologists and going to various support groups we finally got more valid answers to our questions. Cory's psychiatrist, Dr. Singh agreed with part of the above assessment. He said that some people with schizophrenia do have a crisis of identity. They don't have confidence, they aren't sure of themselves, they don't know what they want to do in life and have lots of trouble making decisions. But it's not clear which comes first. Does the onset of the disease cause the confusion and fear, resulting in a loss of identity and self esteem? Or was this personality trait there all along, and it makes the slip into psychosis easier?

Studies show that all people with schizophrenia have an anomaly in their DNA, one gene that's off. If you have this anomaly in your genetic makeup and then experience some sort of crisis (an accident, an abuse, something that puts you into a state of extreme anxiety and fear), this can trigger the onset of the symptoms of schizophrenia, the delusional voices and the visual hallucinations. Your brain chemistry has been altered and the doctors don't think it can go back to normal. This explains why schizophrenia usually appears in young people between the ages of 19 and 25. It's the time when they are finally out on their own, at college or trying to find a job. They are away from the protective umbrella of the family unit and their brains are just ripe for this kind of anxiety and loss of grounding to set in. We have searched our memories for anything that happened to Cory that could qualify as an abuse or crisis and have come up empty.

Of course, the studies also show that not everyone with this anomaly in their DNA will develop schizophrenia. It takes that traumatic event to trigger it. Most people don't have a life-altering trauma between 19-25 and even those that do, and who also have the rare gene, may have enough mental stability to make it through unscathed.

Cory had anxiety from an early age. I remember an episode in 7th grade when he developed a fear of going blind. The class had been reading a book about a boy who lost his sight because he looked at the sun during a solar eclipse. This was the story he was told by his family, but it turned out that his brother, in a fit of jealous rage, had thrown a chemical into his eyes, which had blinded him. The details of the story are not important, even though it was hard for me to understand why the teacher was making 12 and 13 year olds read such a frightening book.

Cory became obsessed with eye protection, wearing sunglasses whenever outside, and he took to checking his eyes, frequently covering one at a time with his hand to make sure they were both working fine. After a few weeks of this his teacher noticed and so did the other students, who started asking him if he was okay and if his eyes were bothering him. He was embarrassed and self-conscious. Finally he decided to tell the teacher what was going on and luckily she was very sympathetic. She sat with him after school for a while and gave him some very good advice.

"If you keep something hidden inside, something you are worried about, and don't tell anyone, it starts to grow. The secret feels bigger and bigger. It becomes like a speed bump that is harder and harder to get over. Once you can let it out and tell someone you trust, it begins to shrink and often it can recede altogether. I'm so glad you came to talk to me about this."

She told Cory to raise his hand if he had a sudden feeling of panic while in class and just ask to be excused. She would let him go to the school psychologist for a chat. Her strategy worked and Cory's anxiety about his eyes went away. He felt he had a trusted ally in school now and an avenue to help.

7. Quickly Changing Moods

For the first seven or eight years after his schizophrenia diagnosis Cory had episodes of intense psychosis each year, and they seemed to come in cycles. At first we thought they were seasonal. As winter approached, and there were shorter days and more darkness, his voices increased. There were also times, even in spring and summer, when the early part of the day was better. As evening came on he would melt down and hear the voices practically non-stop. This is similar to a pattern that elderly dementia patients often experience called "sundown syndrome." I guess it can happen to anyone, especially someone suffering with mental illness.

The look that would come over Cory's face as the voices started torturing him was so painful. His eyes would squeeze shut and his mouth would scrunch up into a grimace. He looked like he was going to cry, and a whine of despair would escape from his mouth, but strangely no tears appeared. It was such a sound of desolation, and a look of hopeless vulnerability. He was obviously feeling something deeply troubling but quick as turning the TV channel, if you offered him a sandwich or a cup of tea, his eyes would clear, he would turn his head to look right at you and with a normal, almost cheerful tone say, "That sounds good. Yes, please!"

What is this phenomenon of the brain that can cause a person with schizophrenia to jump back-and-forth between delusional pain and comforting reality? Sometimes when Cory had been in a scary delusional state for a long time and then came back to present reality, the delusions seemed like dreams to him, vaguely remembered, hazy and far away. We tried not to speak of them, to keep them in the realm of non-reality, distant. But when Cory was in this in-between state, bouncing back and forth quickly between annoying voices and present reality, this was the time when he felt the most angry and frustrated.

He wanted to be in the normal world, but the voices kept intruding and confusing him. He felt tortured and wanted them to stop but, like annoying bullies, they wouldn't shut up. How does one handle being bullied? What is the best tactic if you can't get away from them? Cory tried giving in to them, doing what they demand but then they only demand more. If he tried to ignore them, they threatened dire consequences and he would worry that he wouldn't be able to sleep. The night time was the hardest time. There was no one to talk to, no one to distract him. He was alone in his room with silence all around, just ugly, mean voices talking, ranting and threatening in his head. That our son managed to retain any of his blessedly cheerful good nature is a miracle.

Since the voices began we have tried many approaches to bedtime and helping Cory get to sleep. Every night we put on a meditation from a free website called "*Fragrant Heart*" which has many different meditations for healing, compassion, health, stress etc. If that didn't do the trick, Eric or I would sit on his bed and sing quiet songs and say comforting prayers. Hearing our voices helped to blot out the internal ones in his head. Thanks to this, plus the medication, he would eventually drift off.

When the psychosis was at it's worst Eric or I would sleep in the room with him on the futon couch. Multiple times during the night Cory would raise his head and go up on one elbow to check that we were still there in the room. He did not feel safe unless we were there. This happened more in the beginning, the first few years, when he still was not convinced that the voices weren't real. In the middle of a psychotic episode it is so hard to tell the difference between delusion and reality. Dr. Singh, Cory's psychiatrist, has tried to get us to understand that the delusion becomes the reality. And when Cory is in a delusional state, to deny his reality is very scary and frustrating. Over the years the best advice, given to us by our sister-in-law, Maryrose, a psychiatric nurse, was:

1. Be as calm and loving as possible. Show no frustration or anxiety. Do not engage in talk about the voices because that will only make them seem more real. Be sympathetic without mentioning the voices and what they are saying. Instead, say something like, "You look so scared, or sad. I'm here to help."

2. Redirect his attention to something else. "Let's go get a cup of tea and sing a song at the piano."

In the beginning we tried so many things that were completely the wrong approach. But what did we know? We tried reasoning with Cory. "No one else hears those people. Look outside. There is no one out there. You are the only one who hears them. They are just chemicals in your brain that sound like a radio." This approach just made him angry. We didn't believe him, we didn't understand and it made him feel that he couldn't even trust us! During one of his worst episodes he actually packed a bag at 2:00 AM and went and sat on our porch; the voices had told him they would come in a red RV to pick him up and take him to safety. (You see, there are good voices as well as bad ones.) The only way I could think of to get him back inside the house, after he had waited for an hour and of course they hadn't come, was to tell him that I would tape a note on the front door saying, "Please come back in the morning, I will be ready to go at 9:00." It worked and got Cory back to bed, but it also affirmed to him that I, too, believed the voices were real people.

After this episode Dr. Singh decided it was time to switch medications again. We had tried several atypical antipsychotics that work well for most people. They were *Risperdal, Seroquel, Zyprexa and Saphris*. But all of them except *Seroquel* had been ineffective for Cory and even *Seroquel* seemed to lose its efficacy over time and needed to be increased constantly. Cory had reached the maximum dose of 1200 mg. per day, so Dr. Singh decided it was time to try an old, reliable medication called *Haldol* in conjunction with *Seroquel*.

The American Psychiatric Association recommends that psychiatrists follow a proscribed set of steps in regard to medications. These steps include trying a number of different categories of antipsychotics, including newer and older ones, often referred to as *atypical* and *typical*. We had heard of a relatively new medication called *Clozaril* that was supposed to be extremely effective at reducing the symptoms of schizophrenia. Because *Clozaril* carries the risk of a rare but very dire side effect, this medication requires regular blood monitoring. Patients without a lot of support often cannot manage the daily, weekly and monthly blood tests that are necessary to watch for this life-threatening side effect. This extra blood monitoring step was the reason that *Clozaril* was the medication of last resort and why psychiatrists are expected to try all of the other categories of medications before moving on to *Clozaril*. Since we had not yet tried any of the older medications, Dr. Singh decided *Haldol* was the best next step.

8. The Haldol Years (2014 – 2015)

After Cory had been on Haldol for a few months, just getting out of bed in the morning was a trial. His body was so stiff that he could barely move his legs. It seemed like an immense effort to connect his brain to his limbs. His feet dragged heavily across the floor as he painstakingly made his way to the bathroom in his walker. Naked, his twisted body looked almost S-shaped, a backward S. His shoulders were so rounded, his stomach protruded and his knees were bent in a half crouch. Just stepping over the three-inch lip into the shower stall took such an effort of concentration, and hanging onto the grab bars took every ounce of strength that he had. Once he was seated and the shower was going I watched through the frosted glass, droplets of water trickling down and steam wafting out the opening at the top of the door. He would often sing a song: "When you're alone and life is making you lonely, you can always go… Downtown." I would see him lean into the stream of water, letting it pour over his head and then start to scrub the shampoo into his scalp. He always forgot the back of his head so usually that didn't get any shampoo, but it was clean enough. "Don't forget your pits and your butt," I would yell. He would answer dismissively, "Yes, Mom."

This was our usual refrain, so boring and familiar, repeated every shower. Then the water would turn off with a clunk, the door would pop open and he would call out, "I'm done!" I would dry him off with a fluffy teal-blue towel, his favorite color, as he stood shivering, holding himself up by clinging to the bars outside the shower stall. Then it was back to his room to get dressed. He needed help with everything during this period, shirt, pants, shoes, socks and orthodics. He would still proudly put on his own deodorant though. The whole process could take up to an hour and was exhausting for him. How did he manage to be so patient and retain his sense of self? Or was he slowly losing it, piece by piece, with each job he gave up, allowing someone to help him, or do it for him?

Towards the end of the Haldol phase, Cory had become so weak from inactivity and sedation that he could not keep his balance, even while

sitting. He would start tipping to the side and eventually fall over if someone didn't prop him up. The couch in his room has no arms and this next episode took place during that time.

"I hate having CP! I want to chop it up and put it in the dog's breakfast. It stops me from doing the things I want to do!" he sobbed. He clenched his fists and howled, "Why me? Why do I have CP?" We watched, aching to help, as our son tried to laboriously haul himself up from the floor after falling sideways off the couch. His twisted legs were so weak and atrophied but he screamed, "Don't help me! I can do it myself!"

He was panting with the effort, straining to turn onto his hands and knees and crawl to the couch, trying to raise himself with just the strength of his arms. But he had gotten so big and so sedentary that he couldn't lift himself up anymore and finally he conceded and let us grab him under the arms and lift him up onto the couch. He looked like a wounded bear, hunched over, eyes red and filling with tears. Oh, the unfairness of it! To lose the little mobility and independence you have at such an early age. 25! Too young to be so old.

One night I dreamt that I was protecting Cory from an abusive woman. Dreams come from our own minds and a friend once told me that her therapist said everyone and everything in your dream is you. Even that toaster she dreamt about, bursting into flames, was her in some way.

In this dream I was protecting my son, rushing into the room when I heard him screaming. A woman was hitting him and I tried to tear her off of him. She was hurting him and I yanked and pulled at her with Amazonian strength. But was I the abusive woman too? I had gotten so frustrated with him, or to be more truthful, with his psychosis, the irrationality of it and the bitter frustration and anger that my son was no longer the person I knew. He had changed. He was delusional. He talked of wanting to be a *corrections officer* in a prison, the worst, most inappropriate job for him. He would buy thousands of dollars worth of ladies handbags and then they would end up unused in his bedroom closet, or strewn around the house, hanging off the backs of couches and chairs. I made many snarky comments and groaned when he came back from TJ Maxx with yet another wasted purchase. (Believe it or not, even during this time, when Cory was the most debilitated, he still had the determination to go shopping. He would hobble to his electric scooter and ride on it, downtown, listing to the side, looking like a ninety year-old geezer. His coordination was so poor that once he drove off the sidewalk and tipped over. He lay trapped under the weight of the scooter until a neighbor passing by came to help him. His judgment was so impaired that it was scary. I often felt compelled to drop everything I was doing to go with him as protection, but this only added to my frustration.)

At times I couldn't contain my anger. Once in the middle of the night he got up on feet that had, just days before, been in such pain that he couldn't walk at all, and in his bare feet came and woke us up saying his feet hurt. "Why are you out of bed, walking on them, then?" I said, as I rolled my eyes. "Not the greatest idea, Cory...."

But then his eyes would fill with tears. He knew in some corner of his brain that he was not thinking clearly but somehow could not wrap his mind around a rational thought. I knew I had wounded him and hurt his fragile confidence even more and so then I would pull myself together and try to be kind and patient. I have two sides to me also and sometimes I wondered who is more the schizophrenic, Cory or me?

As I told this dream to my husband Eric the next morning it dawned on me that there is another interpretation of the abusive woman in the dream. The voices that Cory hears in his head are almost all women, he says. And most of them are very abusive. Eric and I could spend half the day defending him from the horrible things they say. I have tried every trick in my arsenal: to reason with him and if that fails to simply distract him with card games, letters to write, songs to sing together, or sometimes an outing to the mall or grocery store. So yes, I might be the abuser sometimes but also the protector. And if I'm everyone in my own dream, am I also Cory? Perhaps I too, feel abused by this situation, by the voices in Cory's head. I have felt like a woman trapped in a life she never wanted, a life that prevented her from living the life she had hoped for.

9. Observances of a Butterfly

My eyes are made of light blue marbles and I look down on the bedroom scene below. I'm a butterfly, a ceiling ornament, made of plastic, with large spotted yellow and black wings. I'm hanging from a large hook above the boy's bed and I can watch everything. The bird's-eye view is so clear. It's a family drama, a sad story really, but one that has equal parts love and tenderness and agony and frustration. I am very objective. I've seen lots of episodes unfold here, but what I see tonight is so personal and heartbreakingly sad. The boy has begun to descend into a delusional state. He mumbles about going downstairs, that something bad will happen if he stays up here in bed. The clock says 1:00 AM. The mother has come in and is trying to talk sense into him.

"There's nothing to be afraid of, you can go down and sit in the La-Z-Boy in the morning. I'm right here, I can stay with you in the room if it makes you feel safer." She sings him bits and pieces of a song from *Phantom of the Opera*, "No more talk of darkness, forget these wide-eyed fears. I'm here, nothing can harm you, my words will warm and calm you."

I stretch my plastic wings and sigh. I've seen this scene many times over the months and years, sometimes with the father who calmly and gently sits with the boy. Maybe he felt sick or anxious and the father has heard him cough. Like a bolt of lightning he is in the room, holding the bucket under his son's chin to catch the vomit. And then tucking him tenderly back in under the covers. He will sit on the couch as the boy falls back to sleep, reading or just thinking his own thoughts, a comforting presence as the boy drifts off to sleep again. Tonight the mom sings the song.

"I'm here, with you, beside you,

To guard you and to guide you."

She gives him another pill and she warms his bed-buddy in the microwave and strokes his hair, whispering the gentle, comforting words of a favorite prayer by Saint Theresa. Then, when his eyes begin to close, she sits on the couch, huddled up and chilly, hugging her knees because she forgot to bring a blanket in with her. For 20 minutes she waits. Will he wake again and be afraid? He lifts his head once or twice to check that she is still there, watching over him and then, when she thinks he's asleep, she tiptoes out and back to her own bed, which has turned cold.

She lies awake for a long time thinking, "What are we in for this time? What will I do when Eric goes on tour? How can I handle this by myself? Will it be as bad as last time?"

But then at 2:30 he's up again, scraping across the floor in his walker, as slow as a snail, trying to sneak downstairs without waking up the old folks. But no! They hear him as he reaches the top of the stairs and this time they both come out. "Where are you going? It's the middle of the night! Why are you going downstairs?" His face contorts. He doesn't want to tell them. He knows they don't believe him. He grimaces in pain or sadness. "I've got to get downstairs. They are coming to rescue me," he thinks to himself. But all he can mumble is, "I don't know, I don't know."

"What don't you know, sweetheart?" the woman asks. "I don't know, I don't know." She tries to soothe him, speaking gently and with a forced calmness, trying to mask the anxiety she is feeling.

As I look down at them I wonder, is it going this way again? Are they in for another episode of delusional nights, filled with escapades down and out into the street? Hours of waiting for imaginary people to appear, red RV's coming to take him to safety? More and more drugs that turn this young man into a drooling zombie?

The woman waves her husband back to bed. "You sleep, you have to work in the morning. I'll stay up with him." They disappear down the stairs and turn the TV on. Infomercials! That's all that's on at 3:00 AM. The toaster clicks and pops. She must be making him something to eat, toast or a muffin. The microwave whirrs, maybe a cup of warm milk and honey? They do that sometimes. It helps him settle back to sleep.

After an hour or so the wheelchair bumps over the kitchen threshold and I hear the hum of the stair-chair carrying the boy up to the 2nd floor. She gives him more medication, warms the bed-buddy in the microwave in his room, and gently helps him into bed. Her eyes are glazed and her voice strains to sound patient.

"Go back to sleep my love; everything will be better in the morning."

"Say the prayer again, Mom, please," he whispers, and so she begins.

"May today there be peace within. May you trust you are exactly where you are meant to be. May you not forget the infinite possibilities born of faith in yourself and others. May you use the gifts you have received and pass on the love that has been given to you. May you be content with yourself just the way you are. Let this knowledge settle into your bones and allow your soul the freedom to sing, dance, praise and love. It is there for each and every one of us."

His eyes have closed and she silently sneaks back to her room, next to his, but sleep eludes her. She lies awake for a long time. Finally she reaches for her own angel-of-sleep medication and waits for the curtain of blankness to lower her into a dreamless rest.

Back in the boy's room I think how often I've seen this scene play out, and wonder to myself how I got so lucky to be able to watch such a poignant family drama, with many episodes, when most ceiling ornaments have nothing to entertain them in the long hours of the night.

10. OCD and Bags

The rage that starts to percolate and bubble inside becomes so strong that it bursts out in an uncontrollable eruption of yelling!

"Fuck it!" I yell. "I don't care about your bags! Do whatever you want but I'm going to bed!"

I hammer my fists against his closet door, slam it shut with a loud crack and run from the room, crashing that door behind me. Collapsing onto my bed, my heart racing and breath coming in fast gulps, I feel disgusted with myself. How can I let my frustration get away from me like that? What kind of a mother am I?

I have a son who spends hours at a time fiddling with his collection of purses and wallets and keys, always switching, changing, asking for help. He's ill! Yes, I know, but it still drives me crazy. It's a feeling of being trapped inside a recurring nightmare, or more like a room with no air, and hidden walls that confine me and close me in, even though I can't see them. But why not just calmly walk away and leave the scene, go read quietly in my room? Why the compulsion to stay, to argue, to try to reason with someone who can't see reason? There is no reasoning with obsessive-compulsive disorder or schizophrenia! He must do this ritual, no matter how late, no matter how tired, or he won't be able to sleep.

And that's my worry: If he doesn't sleep, neither will I. So that's the catch. I want to sleep, I'm tired, I can't wait to get into bed and disappear into a good novel, away from this life of perpetual compulsions, paranoia, anxiety and delusions, which is my son for the last several years. And so I lie on my bed thinking;

"I must be more patient. I cannot let my anger and frustration show. It only aggravates the situation and it accomplishes nothing."

And then as my breathing slows and my heart stops its bouncing and pounding, I hear a sweet voice from the other room.

"Are you feeling better now Mom? Did that help?"

Angel, I think. He's an angel....

11. The Hills Are Alive!

Sometimes when the voices in Cory's head are very bad, we suggest he sing. Either we turn on some music and sing along or we will go to the piano and I will play while he sings. He sings loudly. The loud piano and his own loud voice, when combined with reading or remembering the words, is sometimes enough to drown out the voices in his head. It engages his brain in multiple ways that leave little space for the voices to break through. But one time, when his psychosis was particularly bad, even that couldn't prevent them from busting in. It became almost comical.

Cory was singing along with his voice teacher, Cheryl, the title song from the Sound of Music that begins with "The hills are alive." It is such a beautiful, touching song about nature, love and music. Unfortunately, it wasn't ideal for this purpose because each phrase comes to rest with a two-beat pause before continuing. That was just enough time for Cory's brain to rest also and for the voices to pop in. He struggled to keep the voices away by answering them back in the pause and it was actually very funny. It sounded something like this:

"The hills are alive with the sound of music," ....("Not going to happen!")

"With songs they have sung for a thousand years," ....("I don't think so!")

"The hills fill my heart with the sound of music," ....("Shut up already!")

"My heart wants to sing every song it hears." ....("No, you can't make me!")

We've laughed about this episode many times and in our family we think of the voices as annoying, pesky, bothersome entities that threaten and harass but actually have no power unless you give them attention. "They have no arms or legs," we are constantly reminding Cory. "They are just sounds in your brain like a radio station you can't turn off, that spouts conspiracy theories and wants to make you afraid." We tried to tell him to use the technique that worked when the bullies in third grade stole his potato chips at lunch. The only thing that made them stop was to ignore them and pretend he didn't care. If you talk back to them or yell at them to stop, it only encourages them and makes them more real and gives them more power.

Here is a flashback to the story of the "Potato Chip Wars."

12. *Potato Chip Wars*

Cory has always loved potato chips; salty, crispy and oily, they go perfectly with a sandwich and a juice box, and this is what I packed for his lunch almost every day when he was in grammar school. Maybe I'd toss in a few apple slices and a cookie or two for dessert but the potato chips were his favorite part. The other kids that he sat with at the table in the lunchroom knew it, too.

One week in third grade the need to tease or torture someone rose up at Cory's table and he became the unlucky target. I'm not sure if it was really mean-spirited, since they knew Cory couldn't get up and run around the table. Possibly they saw him as equal to everyone else and not disabled. In any case, the boys at the table grabbed his bag of potato chips and started throwing them back and forth to each other.

"I've got your chips, Cory, ha ha, come and get them! Oops no! Now Sean has them, oops now Peter has them. Oh, sorry, Cory, now Tommy has them."

That first day Cory never got his chips back, no matter how much he pleaded. "Give them back! Hey, those aren't yours. Please! I want my chips."

After a couple of days of this Cory reported to us what was going on at lunch. Trying to help in my over-eager way, I suggested, "How about I pack chips for the other kids and you can give them their own?"

"No, Mom," he sighed, slightly exasperated, "we're not allowed to share because of food allergies."

"Well, why don't you report them to the lunch-room aide? She will stop them."

"I don't want to be a tattletale, Mom."

Finally Eric, in his usual thoughtful and insightful way, found a solution that Cory was willing to try. "It will take a lot of patience and will-power on your part, Cory," he said, "but I can guarantee it will work in three days. Ignore them. Act like you couldn't care less. Turn to the person sitting next to you. Is it your friend Sophia? OK, just talk to her like you don't even notice or give a hoot."

"When you get home," I chimed in, "you can have all the chips you want."

We even did some practice role-playing, Dad being the mean kids teasing and grabbing his chips. I sat next to Cory pretending to be Sophia, as he turned his head, nose in the air, pointedly ignoring his father while talking to me.

Cory agreed to try it. On the first day the boys grabbed the chips and started tossing them back-and-forth. "I've got your chips, Cory! Ha ha, now Sean has them. Don't you want your chips? Here they are."

I can't imagine what determination it took for Cory to look the other way and not react, but eventually the boys gave up and threw the chips back into his lunch box.

The second day there were threats. "I'm going to take your chips, Cory. Hey look I'm taking them!" But they never actually did. They reached out toward the lunch box but they didn't grab them. On the third day lunch returned to normal. There was no stealing and there were no threats. Cory just ate his lunch in peace, chips and all. Cory wasn't playing their game.

Since then a frequent mantra in our home is: "Attention equals power." Or, as my maternal grandfather was known to exclaim, "The power people have to annoy me, I give them."

When ignoring the voices doesn't work there are other approaches we've tried. The most interesting approach we learned from a TED talk given by a woman named Eleanor Longden, who has schizophrenia.

13. Eleanor Longden

A few years into Cory's diagnosis Eric's sister, Ann, forwarded us a TED talk by a woman with schizophrenia. Her name is Eleanor Longden. She gave a most compelling 14-minute talk about her experience from the perplexing beginning, through the excruciating height of her illness to her eventual recovery. In her talk she explained so many interesting factors, things that exacerbated her voices, and strategies that she eventually employed to work with them and understand them and finally reduce them to a manageable, livable level. I forwarded this TED talk to Cory's psychiatrist because much of what Eleanor had found successful was the opposite of the advice we had been given.

We had been told over and over again that the best way to quiet his voices was to distract Cory and keep him busy with other activities that engaged his brain. We were told that the less he engaged with his voices the better, that paying attention to them gave them more power over him and they would increase in frequency and intensity. To a certain extent this technique worked, but Eleanor's strategies seem to have a lot of value as well.

Eric and I had always felt that the voices Cory heard had to have something to do with his own experiences, anxieties and/or traumas. How could they not? They were coming from his very own brain. And Eleanor, after many years of unsuccessful struggles with traditional strategies and medications that rendered her so drugged and stupefied that she couldn't think straight, had found a psychiatrist who was willing to try something else.

He recommended this strategy; your voices are trying to tell you something. Your voices say extreme things that you know rationally will never happen, but the underlying feeling can be valuable to recognize. It is an exaggeration of an unresolved issue or trauma that you haven't dealt with, or a fear or insecurity. Listen to your voices and try to uncover what is the underlying expression. Make a time every day to sit quietly and listen and learn for 30 minutes or so. Don't give them too much time but thank them afterwards for teaching you something about yourself.

Eleanor started to understand that when her voices said, "She should not go out or she will be arrested," it meant she was anxious about being out by herself in the community. If they said, "Her parents are going to be killed," it meant she was scared to live away from her parents. Who would take care of her if they were not there? They reminded her of various other normal anxieties of young adults, worries about her health, never finding a partner or soul mate and worries about sex.

We tried to get Cory to think about his voices this way, too, and the combination of both the traditional and Eleanor Longden strategies seemed to help him the most. It wasn't healthy to spend too much time listening to them, so keeping busy was very important, but it also wasn't healthy to ignore such an integral part of yourself completely.

14. Heart Disease, GERD and Nagging

Before the schizophrenia diagnosis Cory was actually trim, you might even say skinny. But the medications that he is taking have caused tremendous weight gain. The doctor explained to us that these antipsychotics do two things: they increase your appetite while at the same time slowing down your metabolism, so it's inevitable that someone taking them will gain weight. Therefore, patients on these drugs for a long time will frequently develop diabetes and/or heart disease. Great! Also, the meds increase the chance of acid reflux and gastric bleeding and stomach ulcers.

So now you have another whole set of worries, and doctors who prescribe more medications to address these issues. It's no wonder that Cory (and his voices) talk about fear of dying or getting sick. The doctors all have their suggestions: Less red meat, fat and sugar to get your cholesterol down. Limit your coffee to reduce the GERD. But Cory was in his twenties and didn't want to be limited. He paid NO attention. So I became the awful, nagging, helicopter-mom even more, worse than Amanda Wingfield in the "Glass Menagerie."

"You drink too much coffee! It's bad for your GERD! Sit up straighter. Slumping like that in your chair is bad for your internal organs. It's no wonder you have so much acid-reflux. All that sugar! You're going to become a diabetic!"

I have said all these things to my son and then felt absolute rage when he would go to Starbucks and order a huge coffee, a triple grande toffee-nut latte with a side order of peanut butter cups, just a week after a blood test that showed he's pre-diabetic. I even said awful things to him like, "Don't expect me to visit you in the hospital when you have to go on dialysis or have a couple of toes amputated."

At times all I could do is retreat to my room and bury my face in my pillow and howl a muffled cry of frustration. I knew Eric and I would inevitably be the ones to get up in the middle of the night to clean up his vomit when the reflux bubbles up at 2:00 AM. We will be the ones to change the sheets and put the dirty ones in the washer at 3:00 AM and we will be the ones who go back to bed at 3:30 and lie staring at the ceiling, unable to sleep, feeling angry, sad, burdened and wondering how to care less.

Having your first and only child be born with Cerebral Palsy, both Eric and I had jumped in head first to the role of fixers. Therapy in Hackensack three times a week, and therapy at home every day. We had our routine down to the minute: up at 5:30 AM, shower and dress, stretching and strengthening exercises with Cory from 6:00-6:30. Then breakfast, and out the door to school and work at 7:20. We kept this up throughout his school years, from preschool through high school.

We also hired tutors to help him with his schoolwork and we bought adaptive tricycles so that he could get exercise. We had all sorts of therapy equipment at home, bolsters and inflated balls to roll and stretch on. Our living room was more like a gym. We even hung a platform rope-swing from the ceiling for Cory to practice balancing and to strengthen his core muscles. So as you can imagine, it was hard for us to stop feeling we had to be in charge. We had directed his daily activities for so long. Eric got there well before I did.

15. Loosening the Reins

I think the light dawned on me one day about eight years into his schizo-phrenia. It really did take me that long! Up until then Eric and I had dif-fering strategies. I don't know if it's a male/female thing but Eric was able to be so much more detached and objective about Cory's health issues. He kept saying, "He needs to learn how to take care of himself, even if it's the hard way by having some problems. If he eats too much greasy food he'll get heartburn, he'll be uncomfortable. If he watches scary police shows on television they will rev up the voices. If going on dating sites and meeting strange, weird men who only want sex revs the voices, he will learn which sites are more friendly and less kinky."

But when these things happened all of us were affected. Cory fre-quently got sick in the middle of the night from over-eating or drinking soda right before bed. Watching a police drama, and even some of the more moderately funny police shows like *Rizzoli and Isles*, could set the voices off. He would then be talking about arrest and prison for days and we would have to listen and try to reassure Cory over and over that this was not going to happen to him. And the more he went on dating sites, the more the voices started talking about rape.

So my tactic was to discourage him from doing all those activities that would increase his delusional voices. The epiphany came to me when Cory, after an unusually tense conversation, finally yelled,

"I can't live my life, Mom, being afraid to do anything that might rev the voices. Sometimes the voices say, 'He shouldn't go to that concert, something bad will happen,' or 'If he goes out, his debit card will be stolen and he won't be able to buy anything.'

"When they say those things, you tell me not to give in to them, that they have no power. Nothing they say is going to come true. But when you want me to stop looking for a boyfriend on the dating site, and when you want me to stop watching my favorite TV shows, isn't that giving in to them and letting them have power over me?"

The more he talked the more I realized that Cory had gotten to a point in the progression of his illness where he actually understood how to deal with his voices and had strategies that worked to combat them. I loosened my tight grip on the reins.

In the area of food, Eric and I made a pact. Cory was, and still is, craving fatty, salty, greasy carbs and meat. So Eric and I tell him if he wants something other than the healthy food that we provide, either at home or at a restaurant, he must pay for it and go get it himself. And that usually works. As a dependent disabled adult he gets a small stipend from the government but he doesn't want to blow it all on food. Plus, it takes a lot of effort to get on his scooter and go pick it up himself. I can count on one hand the times he was determined enough to do that. We do relent and go get it for him on occasion and Eric is more of a softy than I am.

16. The Sun

We all need light in our lives. I'm not just speaking of the reality of sunlight but lightness of being, hope and happiness. But let's start with actual sunshine. We had the experience with my mother, as she aged, and with Cory, that sunlight made a huge difference to their mental health.

I am definitely a morning person and I can feel a distinct lift in my mood as soon as the sun comes up. I might have been tossing and turning just hours before, unable to sleep, but as soon as I throw back the curtains in my window I feel more able to handle whatever I am going to have to face that day. Seeing the sun beginning to peek through the clouds and the birds nesting in our corner gutter, swooping back-and-forth from the house to the tree to the telephone line, I feel the anxieties evaporate with the morning mist.

In the fall of 2016 Cory began to spiral down, his psychosis rearing its ugly head again. He had been on Haldol for two years by then. The side effects were extreme. Not only would Cory turn into a zombie, his head drooping and saliva trickling out of his mouth and down the side of his face, but he also had loss of motor function. After a while he was unable to walk without a walker, especially in the morning. It became hard for him to dress himself. When sitting on the couch he would slowly start tipping to the left side and would end up slumped over on his side, unable to right himself. And in spite of all these sedating side effects, the Haldol did not get rid of the voices!

As winter came on the delusions grew worse. His voices became more and more aggressive and belligerent. As before, the evenings were the most difficult. The dismal process of his daily fight with them seemed to worsen around four or five in the afternoon, as it grew dark. It was a fight for the whole family, how to keep Cory distracted enough to blot out the voices. We would sing at the piano, play card games (loud active ones, not quiet thoughtful ones) and get him to write letters to friends and family, although during the *Haldol* years his coordination was so bad that his handwriting was barely legible.

We blasted music from the speakers in the living room or told him to call his cousins, aunts, uncles and friends, anyone to be a real voice to listen to. But nothing really helped for long. For a time we even considered taking him to Florida in the winter to see if longer days and more sunshine would make a difference. This daily battle went on all through the winter and into the spring, and each time we saw the psychiatrist he would increase the *Haldol*.

After a while we began to wonder if in fact the *Haldol* was part of the problem. The more he took the less he seemed able to differentiate between reality and his delusions. His poor brain was so numbed, so drugged, that he couldn't push his way out of the fog to even understand who was talking, someone in the room or someone in his head. He did have moments of semi-clarity when he could say to us, "The voices in my head are so loud, so mean. They are saying that I've got cancer or I'm going to go blind." Even then, when on some level he knew they were just in his head, he had no brainpower left to combat them, to think rationally that none of that was true. He often ended up with his head in his hands, tears streaming down his cheeks, covering his ears and begging us to make them stop!

Finally in April of 2017, after the voices had become essentially a nonstop battle every waking minute, Cory began talking about going to the hospital. This had always been the last thing he wanted but it was the only way he could transition onto the medication of last resort, *Clozaril*.

We had heard that *Clozaril* was extremely effective at reducing the delusional voices and other psychoses of schizophrenia. But it was a medication of last resort because of its potential deadly side effects. In rare cases a bad reaction can occur, a rapid decrease in white blood cells, which can leave you unable to fight infection. Once, during the trial period of this medication, a patient died. Now it is a requirement that anyone taking this medication must titrate up very slowly and have blood tests every day for the first week, every week for the next six months and then monthly for as long as you stay on this medication. Cory was desperate enough to try it, suffering through the extended hospitalization required to wean him off the *Haldol* and onto the *Clozaril*, and putting up with the subsequent nuisance of the blood tests.

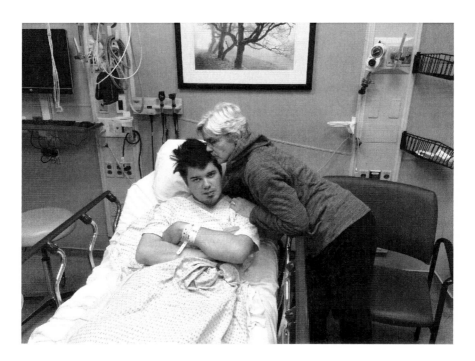

We brought Cory to Englewood Hospital early on the morning of May 16th. After waiting 24 hours in the ER he was finally given a bed in the Voluntary Behavioral Health Unit, known as 4E. It is a small, locked area in the old section of the hospital and it is just one long hallway with rooms on both sides, divided by the nurse's station in the middle. People going in have to speak into the intercom and be buzzed in after explaining who they are and why they are visiting.

The rooms are very small and dark, the only light coming in through high, grimy, grated windows. There were several common rooms, a kitchen where the patients could gather to play cards or grab a snack in between meals, perhaps a package of cookies or some fruit or soda from the fridge. In another room, across from the kitchen, there was a large table where the meals were taken and a morning meeting was held, where patients met with staff to discuss issues and complaints. At the end of the hall was the only moderately pleasant area. This room, open to the hall, had a piano (terribly out of tune) and a couple of couches, chairs and tables for sitting with visitors. It was the brightest place on the unit, with windows on both sides. Although still barred, they at least let in more light than the ones in the small dingy rooms.

Cory spent 11 days in that depressing environment and even had his 26th birthday there. But he stuck it out and was overall very stoic. The nurses were kind, and the assistants who had to help him shower and dress were patient and non-judgmental about a bladder accident in the night. And the best thing, and one of the reasons we chose Englewood Hospital, was that the visiting hours were long, 12:00 PM to 7:00 PM. This is very unusual for behavioral health units, which often only allow visitors one hour per day.

We visited Cory every day for almost all of those seven hours, as did many other family members and friends, bringing him some of his favorite foods to counteract the monotony of the hospital fare. We sat in the visiting area and played and sang at the piano and entertained the other patients and staff with Broadway tunes and church hymns.

Finally, after 11 days, Cory was deemed on the road to recovery and well enough to go home to the care of his parents and local doctors. On the morning that he was scheduled to be released, he sat for hours in a chair, staring at the locked door, waiting for the orderly who would bring the discharge papers and release him to the freedom of the outside world.

Around 2:00 PM on May 26th he said goodbye to the staff and other patients. He said goodbye to the long dreary hallway with the rooms whose doors were never allowed to close, so nurses and staff could check on the patients every 15 minutes, day and night. Goodbye to the smell of old food and of people not very clean and the metallic odor of medication everywhere. Goodbye to the sound of people yelling or crying or babbling to themselves and goodbye to that endless wandering up and down the long hallway in a no-man's land of waiting, endlessly waiting.

It must have felt like a miracle to Cory, to feel the sunlight on his face when we wheeled him out into the parking lot that afternoon. He turned his face up to the sun and reached his arms up to the sky as if by doing that he could gather more of it into himself. His joy at arriving home was palpable. As he stepped out of the car and smelled the grass and rosebushes, sweet and warm in the sun after the rain the night before, he let out the biggest sigh. The birds were busy building a nest in the high gutter of the house, their happy twittering so welcoming. Then, as we turned the corner of the ramp, a laugh of surprise, half joy, half tears, caught in his throat when he saw the "Welcome Home" balloons wafting in the breeze on the front porch, left there by our dear friend, Sue.

Home, Sun, Hope, Happiness.

17. People and Quilts

People are like quilts! This realization came to me as Eric was watching me iron a simple 9 x 9 patch today. He commented on what a transformation happened when I flipped the block over from the underside to the topside. On the underside you see all the raw edges, the seams, the connections, the stitching. Then you turn it over, and Voilà! It all looks neat and ordered, and a beautiful star or geometric pattern is as clear as day. No mess, no straggly threads or uneven edges. It suddenly came to me that people are like that, too. Their outward appearance is often simple and clear. One has no idea what is going on underneath, what messy or complicated work is holding this person together.

Sometimes a quilt is old and worn, tired and faded, a treasured quilt used by many generations, washed a multitude of times, so that the cotton fabric is thin but well loved. You can see that. Or you might see a quilt that has not been well cared for. The dogs or cats have been allowed to chew it, or it's been thrown into the back of a car as a pillow or pad for some animal to sleep on. The insides begin to show. Tears and rips appear and the cotton batting is falling out.

In the Behavioral Health Unit a lot of people are like that. Their stitching is coming apart. Their insides are showing and they have become unraveled. The doctors and nurses and caring family and friends are helping them to patch their holes, add new stuffing and mend the tears and stains and rips, and perhaps put on a whole new backing. The quilt back and stitching is what holds all the insides together with the top of the quilt, the face of the quilt.

When Cory emerged from his hospital stay his insides were on the mend, at least temporarily. The rips and tears, all the traumas that had worn him down until his seams began to fall apart continue to repair themselves with the support he gets from his family, friends, doctors and medication and above all, his own indomitable spirit.

18. Cory has always wanted to be...

It has taken us years to figure out how to respond when Cory tells us what he wants to be when he grows up and gets a job. The list has run the gamut of just about every unsuitable job for a young man with cerebral palsy, and more recently schizophrenia.

Here are some choice examples:

Policeman

Flight attendant

Nurse

Corrections officer

We used to pop his fantasy bubble by trying to reason with him. "Cory, have you ever seen a policeman with a disability? You need to be able to handle a gun, you need to be able to drive a car, you need to be able to wrestle a criminal to the ground and handcuff him. I'm sure there are physical tests you must pass to graduate from the police academy."

But he was not convinced. At 16 he insisted that I take him over to the local police station so he could ask his questions of a real police officer. I am grateful to that kind and gentle young policeman who did not brush Cory's questions aside dismissively. He patiently explained that while he was sure Cory would be able to complete all the classwork and pass the written test, the physical requirements were very challenging. He listed some of them, such as running five miles at a certain pace, lifting a required amount of weight, driving a car, and gun target accuracy.

Cory pestered him with a few more naïve questions. "Couldn't I just be the partner that rides in the passenger seat, handling all the calls? Or perhaps work at the station in the office answering the phones?" These questions the kindly officer answered in depth as well.

After this he focused on being a flight attendant and then a nurse, and luckily we have relatives in both those professions. Eric's brother-in-law, Richard, is a pilot and my sister-in-law, Maryrose, is a nurse. They have both spoken to Cory at length about what those jobs entail and it saddened him to have his fantasy life brought back down to the reality of his limitations.

We have puzzled over his refusal to see himself clearly, to understand his disability and how it is going to affect his life and work. It was frustrating to me that he was so stubbornly attached to these unrealistic fantasies, talking about them for hours, days and weeks on end.

Cory had been a happy child growing up, hardly complaining about his disability and rarely even asking about it. The few times that he did ask, "Why can't I run like the other kids? Why do I have to wear these braces?" we would answer, "Well, everyone has something that is hard for them. Look at grandpa with his stutter, it's hard for him to talk normally. Aunt Sue can't sing to save her life! She is a monotone. You can do anything you set your mind to if you try hard enough."

It seemed easier to play up those half-truths, the pretense that his disability wasn't all that unusual. I've often wondered how much we contributed to his fantasy world when we denied the truth about his disability in his younger years. All his dreams of being a flight attendant or police officer; did we encourage those unattainable goals?

Then, when at 19 the schizophrenia hit, things actually began to make more sense. It took ages for us to come to grips with and understand this illness but gradually we began to see that Cory has always lived in more of an alternate reality. His denial of his disability helped him cope and remain positive, and his fantasies were hopeful.

After the schizophrenia came on we learned that the paranoia that accompanies the delusions is often focused on the police and the fear that you will be arrested, sent to prison or executed. Cory has often said that he wished he could be a policeman because then they would be his friends and know that he was a good person and that he could never be arrested for a crime he didn't commit. That is one of his recurring paranoid fears. He became fascinated with the idea of becoming a corrections officer probably because in his reality it meant he could never be a prisoner.

At one point I listened to a podcast in which the person interviewed was an author, Eliezer Sobel, who has written two books for Alzheimer's patients. Not the caregivers, no…. the patient. He and his wife were living with his mother who had been deteriorating from the disease for many years. His two universal suggestions on how best to cope were:

"Never deny their reality," and

"Connection is more important then memory."

Those two simple but profound truths apply perfectly to our situation with Cory when he is having a delusional episode.

Eliezer had come to realize that sitting with his mother, even if she no longer knew who he was, and reading a simple book with photographs that evoked some feeling or emotion (not even as much as a memory) brought them into connection. They could also share a tender, happy experience dancing together to some familiar but forgotten song or music. His father, by contrast, could not accept his wife's altered reality, yelling at her, desperately trying to reason with her (just the way we used to try to reason with Cory), "OF COURSE YOU HAVE A SISTER! YOU JUST GOT OFF THE PHONE WITH HER FIVE MINUTES AGO!"

Eliezer's mother was a Holocaust survivor. She had escaped Germany at age 14 and had lived her whole life in a state of fear and anxiety. She slept with an ax under her bed in their home in Fairlawn, New Jersey. But Eliezer says that as the Alzheimer's took hold she gradually lost her anxieties and became a much happier and more cheerful person, a loving, childlike and even funny lady.

I think that Cory is also a happier, more cheerful and contented young man when we accept his reality. No arguing, no dismissive shaking of the heads. He often says he wants to rent an apartment and move out, live by himself. Now we tell him, "Call the real estate agency. Find out how much it will cost. Ask if it is handicapped accessible." And he has a great time researching many places and talking to a variety of extremely helpful and friendly sales agents. He is also collecting everything he will need in his new apartment: pots and pans, coffee makers and teapots, mugs and bowls and sets of dishes. He saves up his money for each purchase, and each item requires an excursion down to Kmart or TJ Maxx.

He is happy. He is out in the world, interacting with real people, helpful, friendly people that know him now. The years are passing and he sometimes forgets that he is moving out, that he wanted to be a policeman or a flight attendant. He is living his life. It's not the life we dreamed he would have when he was born, but it's okay for him. He has enough money from the government to be somewhat independent from us, to buy a pizza or go down to Starbucks every day if he wants. He can save up and buy an expensive shoulder bag or coffee maker. His reality and his life are good enough for him.

19. Cory is Back!

I have a candlestick in the shape of a joyful dancing figure, one leg up at a jaunty 90° angle, kicking out with pure happiness, arms raised up toward the sky. The right arm is shooting straight overhead and holds the candle, a torch of light and hope. Even though the candlestick is metal, it appears flexible and is full of movement, leg bent, arms flying up and torso curved in a balancing act on one foot. I love this candlestick! It shouts life. It's shouts hope.

Cory is back! The son we haven't seen for years has now reappeared. Funny, quirky, feisty, stubborn, affectionate, curious, it's all there again. Sometimes it feels like a miracle. The Haldol had buried him in a haze, a fog, in a virtual swamp, unable to think or reason. His movements were slowed to a snail's pace, slumping on the couch and unable to control the saliva drooling out of his mouth. Cory had become a blurry, slow-motion, irrational version of himself, and it caused him extreme anxiety. To feel yourself crumbling, confused and weak, just to try and banish the delusional voices – it raises the question, which is worse? The illness or the cure? No more *Haldol*! This is for sure. There has to be another way and for now it is *Clozaril*, the miracle drug.

There are some downsides to this medication, *Clozaril*. There are side effects. Weight gain is a big one, and GERD (Gastro Esophageal Reflux Disease), which has gotten so bad at times that he has had bleeding in his esophagus and low hemoglobin. His cholesterol has gotten very high and his heart rate fast (tachycardia), so now we have to take him to both the gastroenterologist and cardiologist regularly, in addition to the psychiatrist and the GP. He has to take more medications for these issues. He is up to 10 different meds a day!

So we have traded in his physical health for improved mental health. But he doesn't feel bad if he stays on all the meds for all the problems. He is enjoying life, a life that may be shorter than a normal healthy person without medications, but better to have a happy shorter life than a miserable longer one. My Dad said the same thing when, after his double by-pass, the doctor put him on a high dose of a beta-blocker. "I'd rather have 5 more years feeling alive then 15 more as a zombie!"

Eric and I still debate our role as Cory's guardians. Should we force him to go to PT again? Should we take away his money and control how he spends it to stop him from buying pizza and French fries and all the unhealthy food he craves? How do we balance our responsibility to take care of him, with his need at 30 for some autonomy? We talk to him all the time about the benefits of exercise and healthy eating but we cannot bring ourselves to cut off his income.

What we didn't count on was that after several surgeries, the first to prevent his hip dysplasia and another to straighten his turned-in legs, he would eventually get frustrated and tired of working so hard to stay mobile and fit. Then the combination of the mental illness, which rendered him catatonic for 16 days, and the sedating medications have completely taken away all his motivation to do anything physical. It takes so much energy for him just to get through the day now, getting dressed, showering, going to the post office or Starbucks or Trader Joe's. This is all he can manage, and that's after sleeping 12 hours every night, and often an afternoon nap!

Cory is Back!

Amazingly, Cory is actually a very positive young man. He gets pleasure from such small things as getting a T-shirt folding device like he saw on the "Big Bang Theory" so he can fold his own laundry. Or getting mail in his PO Box or watching his favorite TV shows for the hundredth time. He owns all ten seasons of the "Little House on the Prairie" series, all seven Harry Potter movies, and he watches them over and over.

Just as important, Cory has gotten his confidence back. Even before the pandemic he began going to the hairdresser again, by himself! He would stop into Marijana's shop, which is conveniently located next to Starbucks, and make an appointment. He even risked having his hair dyed blonde, with a blue streak in front, flexing his independence muscles.

It is taking me some time to adjust to his increasing need to be out from under my hovering helicopter wings. But he made it perfectly clear this year by saying he would rather stay home this summer with caregivers, in sweltering New Jersey, than go with us on vacation to Maine.

And so we plod along, grateful that Cory is mentally stable and happy, and our lives are in a calm and comfortable spot at the moment. A friend of mine, whose son is on the autistic spectrum, once compared life to a raft ride down a river without a paddle. It's such a perfect metaphor. Sometimes you drift along in calm water, enjoying the scene, the warmth of the sun and the people in the boat with you. But sometimes you're hurled into rapids and turbulence, bouncing off rocks and desperately trying to keep control of your boat, calling for help to the people on the shore, our doctors, family, friends and caregivers. If we hit the rapids again, with their help we will hopefully reach another calm spot.

20. Acceptance (2021)

Cory has come so far since his hospitalization to get on *Clozaril* in 2017. Let's see… in the ten years since his breakdown we have never seen him this positive and stable. He can motivate himself to do a project. For years Eric and I and the caregivers would have to do all the thinking and suggesting.

"Why don't you write a letter? Or go out for a scooter ride? Let's play a game of cards or a word game. We could bake something or sing and play the piano." Now he has many projects that he busies himself with each day. He writes two or three letters a day and receives several back. He goes to the post office to buy stamps and chats with the postal workers. He goes to the library and takes out books and DVDs. These he rarely reads or watches, but it is an activity and a chance to interact with the librarians. He goes to the computer and invents questionnaires, which he sends to people.

"What are your favorite foods, TV shows, colors, drinks, girls names, boys names, dessert, fruit, vegetables etc."

Before the pandemic he would go to the store and buy lots of stuff with his restricted allowance ($15 a day), most of which he doesn't need. Now he orders online. He has so many cans of coffee. The cupboards are filled up, stuffed, and every so often I decide a can has gone moldy and I throw it out. But he buys more.

He saves his money up and buys expensive tea kettles, even though he has ten more in the basement. One by one I have given them away to the refugee resettlement program at our church. He buys boxes and boxes of envelopes for his letters. He must have over 1000 envelopes now; they litter the area around his desk, and every so often I try to get them into neat stacks and drawers. But all this is not to complain. I want to show that he is happy and busy and able to keep himself occupied without needing me or someone else to entertain him in order to block out the voices. He can do it on his own now.

In 2018 Cory participated in a job-training program with DVR, the Division of Vocational Rehabilitation. He worked with three different job coaches at Goodwill Industries. He enjoyed the experience, for the most part. He especially liked the jobs where he interacted with other people, answering phones, taking donations and printing receipts, or jobs where he got to use a gadget like a computer, printer or price gun. His ideal job, which he asked his job coach about weekly, would be to work as a receptionist at a nice hotel. He had done this as a volunteer a few summers before the schizophrenia hit. It had all the bells and whistles that he likes, answering phones, transferring calls, making key cards, talking to people, AND there was a coffee machine right in the lobby. Heaven!

In the fall of 2018 and early 2019 Cory worked with a job placement specialist from DVR to actually get a job. They fixed up his resumé (basically all volunteer work) and applied to local stores in our area. We were hopeful that he would be able to get a part-time job. People in our town know and like Cory. He is a very familiar figure, riding around the town on his electric scooter, with its orange flags waving. He stops to chat with anyone walking a dog and keeps treats on our porch to tempt people and their dogs to come up and visit with him. Of course, all that came to an end in March of 2020 with the Covid-19 Pandemic. Hopefully when it is all over we will be able to continue with DVR and the job search.

We know now that Cory will probably hear voices for the rest of his life. Sometimes they are gone for a few weeks but then there will be times when they are around every day. When they do pipe up, their continuous, negative babbling is exhausting for Cory. Imagine trying to focus on a conversation with a friend or watch a program on television while in the background you are hearing a loud, obnoxious radio host interviewing a negative, angry person. Luckily he is able to tell us what they are saying and together we can analyze what that might mean. Does it mean he is anxious or angry or even excited about something? And then often he can dismiss what they are saying and get back to life.

We are also so fortunate to have several wonderful caregivers who are paid through the Personal Preference Program of New Jersey, a  Medicaid program that allows you to hire friends, neighbors or even family instead of hiring through an agency. All of our caregivers have true fondness for Cory and he enjoys spending time with each of them in different ways. Tracy will drive him places, to the mall or out to lunch or dinner. With Nancy, who comes on Tuesdays so I can go to my writing group, he goes around town, to the Post Office, Starbucks and the library, or down to TJ Maxx. He just loves to just sit on the porch with Diana, sipping tea or coffee, showing her all his new purchases. And Maribel has a cute little dog, Max, with whom he enjoys playing. The familiar routines are comforting and keep him stable. Cory is having a good, if very different life than we expected for him. He is content with it and that is enough for now. And Eric and I have adjusted our lives as well. Over the years I slowly replaced the career I had as a freelance musician with activities I could do at home. I still need to be creative and so I quilt, write, garden and bake. I am around the house and available for Cory should he need help. And Eric retired a few years early from his job as a cellist in the New York Philharmonic just to ease the burden of care from my shoulders.

21. Stigma

Ever since Cory was little we have been aware that people often jump to conclusions about someone who is different. Strangers would come up to us on the street and ask questions like, "What happened to his legs?" Cory was peppered with questions from children at school. "What are those things on your legs?" (orthotics) "Why do you walk so funny?" (CP) Cory never really knew how to answer them. We suggested he try to educate them by telling them that it was called Cerebral Palsy but that often just led to more questions. "What's that? Is it contagious? How did you get it?" Cory hated answering because their curiosity was rarely satisfied. What child in grammar school wants to have everyone focusing on his twisted legs and tipsy gait?

When Cory was about twelve we found him a wonderful therapist, Philip Wilson. We had been hoping to find a counselor for Cory who also had a disability and would be able to help Cory deal with all of his questions, worries and frustrations about being different. Philip had had polio as a young man and he was very gentle and kind. He had some very helpful suggestions about how to handle the never-ending questions that kept arising. Instead of answering all their questions or ignoring them, which is what Cory tended to do, he told Cory what had worked for him.

"Tell them, 'That's just the way I am.' And repeat that, however many questions they ask."

It worked for Cory and eventually the curious questions stopped.

One summer at a music festival a cleaning lady noticed Cory's crutch and orthotics. Assuming that he had had some kind of accident and broken bones from playing soccer or football, she asked, "What happened to you?"

When he answered, "That's just the way I am," she replied, "If that's the way God made you, then God bless you!" He has always remembered that refreshing answer.

By the time Cory was in grammar school it was clear to us that many people would assume that because he had a physical disability he was also mentally impaired. Cory only began to walk at age four and so we wheeled him around in an over-sized stroller. Even as he got older and was able to push the grocery cart with me, holding on to it for stability, it was clear to others that he had a disability because of his unusual gait. At our local grocery store there was a very well meaning lady greeter who always offered Cory a cookie as we were leaving. Her tone of voice was overly sweet and patronizing. Cory was so put off by her that he never accepted, declining in his very polite but firm way.

"No, thank you, I'm not really hungry."

Cory's third grade teacher was an older woman, near to retirement age. I happened to be in the classroom the day that it was Cory's turn to lead the Pledge of Allegiance. I was appalled at how she spoke to him, so loudly and so very slowly, drawing out each word with an exaggerated clarity of pronunciation.

" CORY, CAN YOU COME UP TO THE FRONT OF THE ROOM, PLEASE. PUT YOUR HAND ON YOUR HEART AND START THE PLEDGE."

Afterwards I asked to speak to her in the hallway and tried to explain that, although he had a physical disability, there was really nothing wrong with Cory's hearing or comprehension.

As a teenager Cory has always carried cross-body shoulder bags, which contain all the items he feels he needs with him, such as wallet, keys, sunglasses, handicapped placard, frequent buyer cards etc. The cross-body bag leaves both his hands free, one to use the *Lofstrand* crutch that helps stabilize him as he walks and the other to open doors or grab railings when climbing stairs. After Cory discovered his new identity as a gay male he began carrying more and more feminine-looking shoulder bags to high school. At one point his guidance counselor actually suggested he leave his bag in her office as it might be cause for teasing or ridicule from the other students. Cory declined, saying, "I'll keep it with me." But her response to that was, "Ah, no! I want you to fit in," and she insisted he leave it in her office.

When Cory started hearing the voices and didn't yet understand that they weren't real people, we tried to make our home a safe place for him to talk about all that was going on in his head. But as the voices grew louder and more frightening, he might blurt out to anyone who would listen that "people" were saying scary things about him.

"People are saying I'm going to be put in jail! They're coming now to arrest me."

I saw the puzzled, uncomfortable looks of the staff at my Mom's assisted living facility when they heard him talking like this and I tried to stop him, saying,

"You really should only talk to me and Dad about this, Cory. Nobody else understands."

Even now, when Cory is out in public and wants to share what the voices are saying to us, or a caregiver, we encourage him to speak in code. He will say,

"Do you want to hear what my friends are saying? My friends are saying that I'm going to lose my wallet today."

Our country has a long way to go before most people can feel comfortable around a person with a disability, be it physical or mental. As much stigma as there is still surrounding the LGBTQ community, even more taboo is any talk of mental illness or substance abuse. When people hear the word schizophrenia they picture a violent, raving lunatic, a very dangerous, uncontrollable person. That is only one extreme end of the spectrum. Anyone who meets Cory will think the opposite. He is a funny, sociable, polite young man who happens to hear delusional voices occasionally.

When Cory is at his worst, in the middle of a severe psychotic episode, he will retreat. He becomes very anxious and sad, frustrated or scared, but never aggressive. He just wants to be protected and kept safe. He is in no way a danger to himself or anyone else. Luckily he has not had one of those episodes in many years.

22. *Finding the Right Doctor*

Over the course of his 30 years Cory has had many counselors, psychologists and psychiatrists. When the voices began in the fall of 2010 he was seeing Philip Wilson, the lovely psychologist we found when Cory was in seventh grade. Philip had a gentle, easy-going approach. He wanted Cory to feel relaxed enough to trust him and be able to open up. A lot of their sessions began with games or small talk, as I remember. As Cory's psychosis began to increase, Philip had the wisdom and humility to tell us that he felt out of his depth and recommended we see a psychiatrist who had experience with delusional voices and could prescribe the right medication.

We liked the woman he recommended. She was older and very experienced but unfortunately she was planning to retire soon. She saw right away that we would be in this for the long haul and it would be better to find someone younger who could follow Cory consistently for the years to come. Again we looked around for a good psychiatrist, and a friend recommended someone close by who had helped her son through some difficult times. Dr. G (I will call him) put Cory on a drug called Risperdal and he was his doctor at the time of Cory's hospitalization for Catatonia. We found him to be extremely unresponsive to our panicked calls for help and guidance during and after the hospitalization. It would sometimes take three or four days for him to return our calls during this very chaotic time of crisis.

We then tried going to the doctor who treated Cory in the hospital (Columbia Presbyterian), but because he was such an important head doctor there, it was hard to get appointments, and he was very expensive.

We asked him if he could recommend someone, perhaps a colleague, who had a private practice nearer to us in New Jersey. This is how we found Dr. Sarabjit Singh.

Dr. Singh has been Cory's psychiatrist for nine years now and he has been the most reliable and responsive doctor ever! He has a very nonintrusive way of assessing Cory's mental status. Since it often makes Cory very anxious to talk about the voices, Dr. Singh gets him to talk about anything, no matter how unimportant. He can tell, when it is hard for Cory to complete his sentences, how many times he has been interrupted by the voices. He also has a simple rating system (zero – five) for how bad are his anxiety, paranoia and voices. It is easy for Cory to rattle off: "anxiety - 1, paranoia - 0 and voices - 2." All this makes the visit to the doctor much less scary.

Cory was actually the first of Dr. Singh's private patients to transition onto *Clozaril*. Because of the complex protocols of regular blood tests, which must be sent to the doctor for approval and then posted on the *Clozaril* registry before each monthly prescription, it took us all some time to get this new system down. We were so grateful that Dr. Singh was willing to undertake this extra burden.

When Cory calls or texts him he usually gets a response within minutes. When I ask for a new prescription Dr. Singh almost always takes care of it the same day and he never minds a pesky little reminder. I remember once texting him, from my kayak in the middle of a lake in Maine, alerting him that Cory was running low on some medication. Five minutes later the jingle of his text came in with his typical, efficient, one-word response, "Done."

He has been exactly the kind of doctor we needed!

23. Addendum

At first Cory was not able or willing to tell us what his voices were saying. Sometimes it was too scary or there were words he was afraid to say out loud, like rape, murder, kill, die etc. He also had a hard time describing the voices, what they sounded like and whether they were male or female. Over time I started jotting down notes of the scraps of information that dribbled out about them and since getting on *Clozaril* he has been able to speak much more freely and coherently about them. Here are some of the things I have learned:

A lot of them have names.

All but one or two are women.

Sarah C is the good voice. She sounds like Mom.

She always wears pink and pink equals protection.

The Jill voice is the alter ego of cousin Jesse.

But there is also a Jessie voice that represents cousin Jesse; she is welcoming and protective.

Maria is a good voice who is funny and plays the piano.

The voice of Dad is much younger than Dad.

The voices speak in code sometimes. Once the voices said Cory should wait in the stair chair because they were coming to take him to safety in a Toyota 4 Runner. "Why a 4 Runner?" I asked. "Because you're running for safety," he answered.

Sarah C talks to the bad voices and tells them to stop bugging Cory. She defends Cory.

She is the only good voice who talks to the bad voices. Otherwise the bad ones talk only to each other and the good ones talk only to each other. Cory says that if Sarah C tells them to be quiet because Cory is tired and needs to go to sleep, they will obey her, but they don't obey when he tells them.

The phrase "going home" is often changed to mean dying or going to heaven by the voices. Therefore Cory avoids using that expression. It makes him nervous and so he prefers to say, "going back to our house."

Cory's voices sometimes say that people are imposters and they have reasons to back it up, such as "Robin never wears pink." They have said Dr. Singh is not the real doctor and Nana is not his real grandmother. They have never said that Mom was an imposter, thank goodness!

Now that Cory is stable on *Clozaril*, he will often text Dr. Singh to let him know when the voices pipe up, and that alone can quiet them down. The doctor explained that knowing that you have support can calm the anxiety that brings on the voices.

Even today, Cory does not like to write the word "die," even if it is just part of another word. When he sends a letter to cousin Jesse, who lives in San Diego, he purposely misspells the city, San Deago. It always seems to get there anyway because the zip code is correct.

Cory says, "Whenever I say I am anxious about something, but don't give a reason, the voices say they are going to give me *Ativan*. This happens with alarming regularity."

When Cory is stressed Sarah C says, "Give me a minute," and she goes to the fire house and runs the siren up and down four times. Each up and down cycle of the siren means the voices have to be silent for three months, so four cycles equals a year. (Of course they never stay silent for that long.) We can hear the siren from our house and Cory often stops to listen to it, hoping it means he might get a break from the voices.

Addendum

Sometimes Cory feels he can control how loud the voices are. He can dial up the good voice (Sarah C) and dial down the bad ones so he has control of what he hears and he chooses to hear the good!

Acknowledgements

This book wouldn't be complete without giving a huge "thank you" to the NAMI (National Alliance on Mental Illness) "Family to Family" support group Eric and I attended. It was a twelve-week course run by trained facilitators who are family members of someone with mental illness. We went every Monday night in the fall of 2014. Not only did the course cover every kind of mental illness, from Schizophrenia to OCD, PTSD, Panic Disorder, Borderline Personality Disorder and Depression, but also brain biology and all different types of medications and their effects on the brain. The course also provided valuable information on communication skills, empathy and self-care for the family members, and resources for fighting stigma. I still have the giant four-inch thick, three-ring binder containing all the information we were given week by week. This is truly a priceless resource, offered to the community for free.

Without the help of our amazing friend Pat, then in her 80s, we would not have been able to attend the NAMI "Family to Family" meetings. She came every Monday night for 12 weeks and kept Cory company, playing card games with him and watching one of her favorite reality shows, "American Ninja Warrior."

Thank you to Lynn Lauber, my writing teacher, for giving me the courage to begin writing, fearlessly, trusting my inner voice and inviting me to her special writing group.

Thanks to the kind and supportive members of that group (Lynn, Joan G., Diane, Bob, Joan O. and Toby) for their encouragement to put these stories together in a book.

Acknowledgements

Thank you to my sister Lindy with her amazing memory and Eliezer, Lynn and Frances for editing, proofreading and invaluable suggestions and encouragement. And to Dr. Singh and Philip Wilson who assured me it was important and valuable.

And thank you, Saint Theresa! Your prayer got us through many a long night.

Most of all to my husband, Eric, who lifted me up when I collapsed in frustration, swept up the hair I had torn out and counseled patience, something of which I have too little. He was my own personal computer guru, who tirelessly read and reread the manuscript and helped with all the editing and formatting technicalities that were so confusing to me.

And to Cory, my dear, brave son; your courage and resilience still astounds me! Thank you for allowing me to publish this book.